BREAKFAST IN *Six*

30 easy vegetarian
and vegan breakfasts

Never more than
6 ingredients

AND JANSEN SCHOUTEN

Table of Contents

Introduction

We created this book with a clear plan in mind — to make breakfast as easy and tasty as possible.

Every recipe in this book uses six or less ingredients. Many recipes are also ready in six minutes or less.

Of course, all our recipes are vegetarian and many are vegan. Many more dairy and egg containing dishes can be made vegan and/or gluten-free. Look out for 'vegan options' and 'gluten-free options' on each recipe page.

We are fully aware that eating a quick, tasty and hopefully nutritious breakfast everyday is not as easy as it sounds. We've learnt through our family lives, and feedback from our wonderful readers on the blog that it is all too natural to fall into a pattern of the same uninspiring breakfasts day in, day out.

We believe breakfast should be enjoyed thoroughly each and every day — without becoming a chore. And so, this book was born. Every recipe you see in here is completely exclusive to the book — it has never been shared on our website before, and nor will it be.

Welcome to
BREAKFAST
IN Six

About HurryTheFoodUp

Otherwise known as Kat, Dave and Hauke, we have been sharing our passion (and recipes) for vegetarian food online since 2014. We firmly believe that the current food industry has gone insane, from awful and avoidable animal farming practices through to an extreme reliance on sugar-laden, heavily processed foods. This book is our answer to help anyone that wants it to take steps into a happier, healthier and more satisfying food life.

Jansen

To do this, we enlisted the help of Jansen, a good friend and incredible head chef hailing from the Netherlands, Europe. Jansen has cooked his way across the world, working in restaurants from New Zealand to Canada to Germany.

His wealth of experience is clear, and each recipe has been individually designed for either maximum taste from wonderful combinations of just six ingredients. Many of the recipes are ready in six minutes or less too — perfect for those busy mornings!

The Recipes

Throughout the book you will come across fabulous food pairings of all shapes and sizes.

Many of these not only work for breakfast — they are knowledge you can take through to lunch and dinner, too.

HurryTheFoodUp strives to be a healthy food website, priding ourselves on providing nutritious meals that have many clear health benefits. The same goes for this breakfast book, and most recipes included are indeed healthy and nutritious. We have also included a couple of 'naughty' recipes — after all, in moderation, we all deserve a little treat from time to time, right?

Every single recipe in this book is vegetarian and seven are vegan, with another nine that can easily be made vegan. That means over half the recipes are suitable for vegans. Unfortunately the food world has many hidden animal products in it, which we will explain in just a moment.

The Ingredients

As mentioned, each recipe uses six or less ingredients.

We know that most people have access to a basic kitchen range, so, for clarity's sake, we have chosen several ingredients that we recommend always having a good stock of. These ingredients are not counted in the six ingredients or less section, and they are: salt and pepper, sugar, olive oil, butter and balsamic vinegar. Each one is integral to many recipes — breakfast, lunch and dinner.

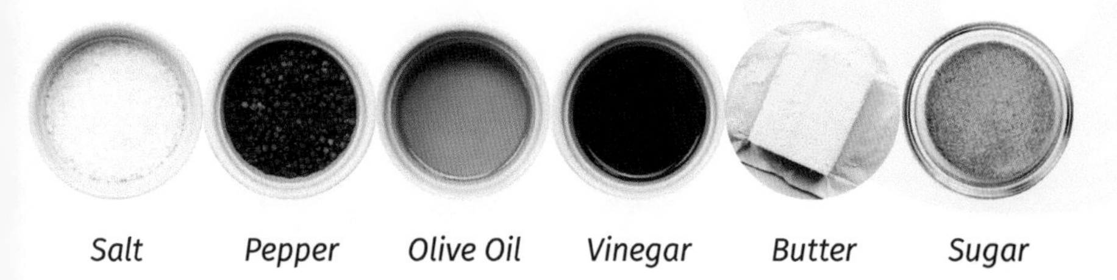

Vegetarian Animal Products

One item that often comes as a shock to people is non-vegetarian cheese. Many cheeses are sadly made with rennet, the juice taken from a baby calf's stomach. Cheeses made this way are naturally not considered as vegetarian, as they include the death of animal to produce them.

We highly recommend checking the packaging of cheese (or asking at the cheese counter) before you buy to see if they include animal rennet. Happily, more and more cheese producers are using non-animal rennet alternatives, so there is a good chance you can still get the variety of cheese you want in a vegetarian way.

It is also worth paying attention to foods that might include these cheeses — pesto, for example. Pesto is usually made with parmesan, a prime user of animal rennet. Again, check whether the jar states if it is vegetarian or not. If it doesn't say, it probably isn't.

Gluten-free

There are gluten-free varieties available of virtually any bread nowadays, if you look in the right stores. If gluten is an issue for you, please don't feel excluded from recipes that use bread — just check your local area for gluten-free alternatives.

THE Recipes

Cheddar and Fig Melt

Vegetarian | Vegan option | Gluten-free option

Servings: 4 | **Total Time:** 10 minutes

Nutrition per serving:	KCAL	FAT	CARBS	PROTEIN
	260	14.5g	18g	15g

Ingredients

4 slices of nice bread

Butter

8 slices of mature cheddar (or similar)

4 fresh figs

2 tbsp fresh thyme (or 1 tbsp dried)

Instructions

1. Heat up the oven to 180°C/360°F.
2. Slice the **figs** and chop the **thyme.**
3. Spread some **butter** on the **bread,** add **cheddar cheese** to each.
4. Put the **figs** and chopped thyme on top.
5. Bake in the oven until golden brown! So good.

Make it vegan

Nowadays you can find various vegan cheese options (even cheddar flavour) in bigger supermarkets. Many of them are really tasty (the cashew based ones are really worth trying).

Make it gluten-free

You can also pick up your favourite gluten-free bread. Whole Foods should definitely have it, so should any bigger supermarket

Jansen's pro tip

If you can't find fresh figs, dried will be fine too!

Mediterranean Pitas with Feta and Honey

Vegetarian | Vegan option | Gluten-free option

Servings: 2 | **Total Time:** 18 minutes

Nutrition per serving:	KCAL	FAT	CARBS	PROTEIN
	222	6.5g	36g	6.5g

Ingredients

2 small pita breads

2 slices of feta (or similar) cheese (finger size thick)

½ cup baby spinach (½ cup = 100g)

2 tbsp honey

2 tsp white sesame seeds

4 slices of tomato

Instructions

1. Preheat the oven to 200°C/390°F.
2. Open up the **pita bread.**
3. In this order, layer over one side: the **tomato slices, baby spinach, feta cheese, honey,** and **sesame seeds.**
4. Let it bake for five minutes in the oven, and don't let the bread burn. Enjoy!

Make it vegan

Use maple syrup instead of honey. To easily recreate the tangy vibe of feta, spread hummus onto the pita and add some black olives. Lovely! (It breaks the six ingredient bank though — naughty.)

Make it gluten-free

The organic food stores and bigger supermarkets are likely to stock gluten-free pita bread. Otherwise you can use any other gluten-free bread for this recipe as well.

Tropical Quinoa Porridge

Vegan | Gluten-free

Servings: 2–3 | **Total Time:** 30 minutes

	KCAL	FAT	CARBS	PROTEIN
Nutrition per serving:	435	21g	60g	8g

Ingredients

½ cup quinoa, raw
(½ cup = 100g)

1 cup water for boiling

¾ cup coconut milk
(¾ cup = 200ml)

2 medium ripe bananas

4 figs

4 tbsp coconut flakes

Instructions

1. Rinse the **quinoa** then boil for 20 minutes in **water.**
2. Drain in a sieve and then put back into the pan. Add the **coconut milk** and bring to the boil again — let it boil for a good minute.
3. Mash the **bananas** and add to quinoa. Leave a few slices of banana for garnish.
4. Cut the **figs** into strips.
5. Put the quinoa into a bowl, garnish with the figs, banan slices and **coconut flakes.**

Jansen's pro tip

You could also cook the quinoa the night before so you can rehea it quickly in the morning.

Indian Parathas with Curried Carrots

Vegetarian | Vegan option | Gluten-free option

Servings: 4 parathas | **Total Time:** 18 minutes

Nutrition per serving:	KCAL	FAT	CARBS	PROTEIN
	108	3g	17g	3.5g

Ingredients

⅔ cup flour (⅔ cup = 75g)

2 tsp olive oil (or canola/ rapeseed oil fits really well here, too)

⅛ cup water (⅛ cup = 30ml)

1 tsp salt

½ carrot, grated

1 bunch parsley, chopped

⅕ cup yoghurt (⅕ cup = 50ml)

½ tsp cumin

½ tsp curry powder

Instructions

1. Mix the **flour** with the **oil,** a good pinch of **salt** and the **water.** Make sure you get a nice soft, but not sticky, dough. Set aside.
2. Grate the **carrot,** chop the **parsley** (leave half for the yogurt) grab a little more salt, the **cumin** and **curry powder** and put it all together in a mixing bowl. Knead a little with your hands to soften up the mixture.
3. Add the leftover parsley to the **yoghurt,** this will be your dip.
4. Make ping pong sized balls from the dough
5. Roll them out flat and add a tbsp of the carrot mixture to the middle. Spread th mixture out across the dough.
6. Fold the dough back over at the edges an make sure the paratha is flat once again
7. Fry the parathas on a medium-high hea for 6–8 minutes, flipping occasionally. Enjoy warm!

Make it vegan

Use non-dairy yoghurt like soy yoghurt to make it vegan.

Make it gluten-free

Just grab a gluten-free all purpose flour mix. There are various brands like Bob's Red Mill or King Arthur who offer it.

Jansen's pro tip

If you run out of curry powder or just fancy a change try using ground coriander instead. It goes really well with carrots!

Crepes with Chocolate and Coconut

Vegan | Gluten-free option

Servings: 2 | **Total Time:** 20 minutes

	KCAL	FAT	CARBS	PROTEIN
Nutrition per serving:	404	14.5g	59g	10g

Ingredients

¾ cup warm water (¾ cup = 200ml)

1 cup flour (1 cup = 120g)

½ tsp salt

1 tbsp sugar

¼ tsp cinnamon

1 tsp coconut flakes

1 tsp cocoa nibs

½ tsp coconut oil

Your favourite spread eg. peanut butter

Instructions

1. Put the **warm water** into a mixing bowl, whisk in the **flour, salt, sugar** and **cinnamon.**
2. Heat up a frying pan (low-medium heat), add the **coconut oil** and gently add the crepes mixture.
3. If necessary, use a soft spatula to spread the mixture out.
4. Make sure it's really thin!
5. Fry it on both sides for 1 minute, don't heat it up too much (pancakes are with colour, crepes stay pale).
6. After you've done that, take it out, put your **favourite spread** on top and fold it twice.
7. Cut it in half, sprinkle the **coconut flakes** and **cocoa nibs** on top and enjoy.

Make it gluten-free

Just grab a gluten-free all purpose flour mix. There are various brands like Bob's Red Mill or King Arthur who offer it.

Jansen's pro tip

The first crepe always sticks to the pan, so be prepared to lose the first one!

French Coconut Toast with Blueberries

Vegetarian | Gluten-free option | Vegan option

Servings: 6 slices | **Total Time:** 18 minutes

Nutrition per serving:	KCAL	FAT	CARBS	PROTEIN
	181	9.5g	20.5g	4.5g

Ingredients

2 eggs

1 tbsp sugar

⅖ cup coconut milk (⅖ cup = 100ml)

1 tbsp butter

4 spoons blueberries, frozen

1 pear

6 slices of brioche bread

Instructions

1. Mix the **egg, sugar** and **coconut milk** together well and let rest for five minutes. Then heat up the **butter** in pan on medium heat.
2. Dip the **bread** into the mixture, then pop it in the pan. Don't dip the bread for long, it'll get soggy! A couple of seconds will do it.
3. After a couple of minutes, flip the bread and cook on the other side.
4. While that's happening, slice some **pear** thinly, and heat up the blueberries in the microwave or small pan. When the bread is ready, lay the pear or plum over it and drizzle on the **blueberries.**
5. Add some **cocoa nibs** if you fancy them. That's it — enjoy!

Make it vegan

Brioche bread is usually made with butter and eggs. A good substitute would be plain white bread. For the butter ideally use coconut oil. For the eggs, use half a ripe banana instead.

Make it gluten-free

You can also pick up your favourite gluten-free bread. Whole Foods should definitely have it, so should any bigger supermarket.

Jansen's pro tip

If you've got leftover ice cream in the freezer, this the place to use it. I love that hot and cold fusion!

Sweet Potato and Parsnip Hash Browns

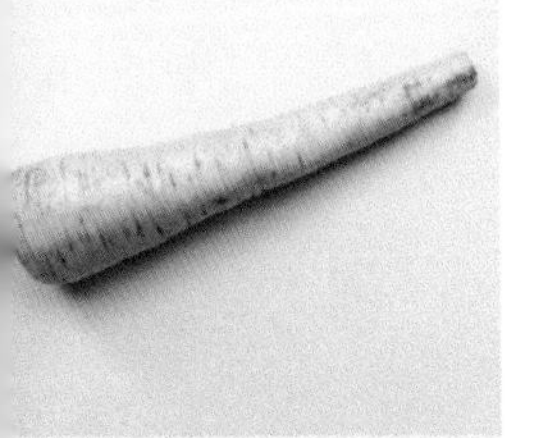

Vegetarian | Gluten-free | Vegan option

Servings: 2 | **Total Time:** 12 minutes

	KCAL	FAT	CARBS	PROTEIN
Nutrition per serving:	313	8g	57g	6g

Ingredients

1 medium sweet potato

1 parsnip

1 tbsp olive oil

2 medium tomatoes

1 tbsp spring onion

4 tbsp yoghurt

6 basil leaves (6 leaves = 1 tsp dried basil)

Instructions

1. Cut the **sweet potato** and **parsnip** into small cubes.
2. Heat up a non stick pan to medium heat with a tbsp **olive oil** and fry them for around 5 minutes, season with a little salt.
3. Meanwhile, cut the **tomato** into the same size cubes. Thinly slice the **basil** and **spring onion.**
4. Add a little bit of **salt** and **pepper,** basil and chopped spring onion to the **yoghurt**
5. When the veggies are soft (not too soft, a bit of a bite is still good), put them on a plate and add the tomatoes. Finish with a good tablespoon of yogurt mix on top. Enjoy!

Make it vegan

Use non-dairy yoghurt like soy yoghurt to make it vegan.

Jansen's pro tip

When it comes to peeling the potato, I go by the skin. If it looks good, leave it on. If it doesn't look appetizing — get rid of it!

Grilled Tomatoes with Blueberry Jam

Vegetarian | Gluten-free | Vegan option

Servings: 6 tomato halves | **Total Time:** 30 minutes

Nutrition per serving:	KCAL	FAT	CARBS	PROTEIN
	75	5.5g	4g	3g

Ingredients

3 medium tomatoes

3 tsp blueberry jam

1 ½ tsp oregano, dried

½ cup grated cheddar cheese (½ cup = 50g)

1 tbsp olive oil

Salt and pepper to taste

Optional

1 handful watercress for garnish

Instructions

1. Preheat the oven to 180°C/360°F.
2. Cut the **tomatoes** in half, and place on a baking tray with aluminium foil or parchment paper.
3. Spread a little bit of **jam** on each of the tomato slices.
4. Then sprinkle **dried oregano** on top.
5. Layer the grated **cheese** ove the tomatoes and place in the oven for 25 minutes or until cheese is golden browr
6. Now garnish each slice with **watercress.**
7. Drizzle with **olive oil** and finish with **salt** and **pepper.** Enjoy!

Make it vegan

Nowadays you can find various vegan cheese options (even chedd flavour) in bigger supermarkets. See what floats your boat.

Jansen's pro tip

These are excellent for a brunch with friends. Double up the ingredients to make sure everyone gets a half or two!

Tangy Arepas with Pomegranate and Lime

Vegan | Gluten-free

Servings: 2 | **Total Time:** 30 minutes

Nutrition per serving:	KCAL	FAT	CARBS	PROTEIN
	290	9g	51g	4.5g

Ingredients

⅖ cup water
(⅖ cup = 100ml)

¾ cup corn flour
(¾ cup = 100g)

1 tbsp olive oil

1 ripe tomato

½ apple

2 tbsp pomegranate seeds

2 tbsp chopped coriander
or parsley

½ lime, juiced and zested

Instructions

1. Mix the **water** with the **corn flour** and the **salt,** stir it until you have a nice soft mixture.
2. Form small balls, about the size of a golf ball.
3. Flatten the balls (to about a finger thick) and fry them in a non stick frying pan on medium heat with **olive oil** until they're golden brown on both sides.
4. Cut the **tomato** and **apple** into small cubes, add the **pomegranate seeds, chopped coriander, lime juice** and **zest.** Season with a little salt and **pepper.**
5. Place the salad onto the arepas and enjoy.

Jansen's pro tip

Use medium heat but adjust as necessary while you're cooking th arepas – we want a nice, golden brown colour, but we don't want to cook too quick and burn. Slower is better.

Fried Chickpeas with Zucchini and Yoghurt

Vegetarian | Gluten-free | Vegan option

Servings: 2 | **Total Time:** 12 minutes

	KCAL	FAT	CARBS	PROTEIN
Nutrition per serving:	433	24.5g	42g	15.5g

Ingredients

1 can chickpeas, drained and rinsed (1 can = dry weight ca. 265g)

3 tbsp olive oil

1 tbsp soy sauce

1 tbsp balsamic vinegar

1 small zucchini

⅖ cup yoghurt (⅖ cup = 100ml)

½ bunch of coriander

Salt and pepper to taste

Instructions

1. Rinse off the **chickpeas,** put them in a bowl and add 2 tbsp of **olive oil.**
2. Take your potato masher (or fork if you don't have one), give the chickpeas a good mashing.
3. Heat up a frying pan and fry the chickpeas for about five minutes, until they have some colour. Add the **soy sauce** and **vinegar** to chickpeas.
4. In the meantime, cut the **zucchini** into thin slices, sprinkle some olive oil on them and grill them for a couple of minutes.
5. You could also use the same pan once the chickpeas have finished. Chop the coriander and add it to the **yoghurt.**
6. Put the fried chickpeas on a plate, and layer the zucchini over the top.
7. Add some **salt** and **pepper** to everythin and drizzle a little yoghurt over to finis Enjoy!

Make it vegan

Use non-dairy yoghurt like soy yoghurt to make it vegan.

Chia Pomegranate Yoghurt

Vegetarian | Gluten-free | Vegan option

Servings: 1 | **Total Time:** 20 minutes

Nutrition per serving:	KCAL	FAT	CARBS	PROTEIN
	306	9g	41g	17g

Ingredients

1 tbsp chia seeds

⅕ cup almond milk
(⅕ cup = 50ml)

2 tbsp raspberries
(frozen or fresh)

¾ cup yoghurt
(¾ cup = 200ml)

1 ½ tbsp elderberry syrup
(or maple syrup if elderberry can't be found)

2 tbsp pomegranate seeds

Instructions

1. Soak the **chia seeds** in the **almond milk** for 15 minutes.
2. If using **frozen raspberries,** use the soaking time to defrost the raspberries. A microwave works great, as does a small pot on the stove.
3. Mix the **yoghurt, syrup,** almond milk, chia seeds and raspberries all together.
4. Sprinkle a few **pomegranate seeds** over the top. Beautiful.

Make it vegan

Swap "regular" yoghurt with soy yoghurt or similar and et voilà — it's vegan!

Mexican Style Breakfast Wraps

Vegetarian | Gluten-free option

Servings: 2 | **Total Time:** 6 minutes

	KCAL	FAT	CARBS	PROTEIN
Nutrition per serving:	379	17g	43g	15g

Ingredients

4 tbsp sweet corn
4 tbsp green peas frozen
3 eggs
1 tbsp olive oil
¼ red onion
1 lime, juiced and zested
Salt and pepper to taste
2 wraps

Optional

Coriander divides camps — if you're a lover, add some to the wraps at the end. If you're not, don't! It's also delicious served with a dollop of creme fraiche or sour cream!

Instructions

1. Fry the rinsed **sweet corn** at a high heat in just a little **olive oil** (be careful, sometimes they like to 'jump').
2. When they're done, throw in the **frozen peas** so they get warm.
3. Whisk the **eggs** and fry them like scrambled eggs in a pan with a little olive oil.
4. In the meantime, dice the **onion,** chop the **coriander, zest** and juice the **lime,** and add everything to a bowl. Add a little **salt** and **pepper** to taste.
5. Roll out the **wrap** and put the eggs on the bottom, layer everything else on top. Roll it up and enjoy!

Optional

Grill the rolled wraps in a pan for a minute — don't let them burn! Otherwise, eat as they are.

Make it gluten-free

You can also pick up gluten-free wraps in selected stores. Whole Foods should definitely have it. If you are unlucky make an open sandwich with your favourite gluten-free bread instead.

Fruity Vegan Smoothies

Vegan | Gluten-free

Servings: 2 | **Total Time:** 2 minutes

1. Mixed Berries Smoothie

Nutrition per serving:	KCAL	FAT	CARBS	PROTEIN
	215	5g	33.5g	9.5g

2 cups soy milk (2 cups = 500ml)
1 tbsp agave or maple syrup
5 mint leaves
1 cup mixed frozen berries (1 cup = 150g)

1. Mix the **soy milk, syrup, mint leaves** and **berries** in a blender. Enjoy!

2. Banana coconut smoothie (vegan)

Nutrition per serving:	KCAL	FAT	CARBS	PROTEIN
	330	14.5g	44g	6.5g

1 cup soy milk (1 cup = 250ml)
1 cup coconut milk (1 cup = 250ml)
2 ripe bananas
1 tbsp agave or maple syrup
1 tsp coconut flakes

1. Mix both **milks, bananas** and **syrup** in a blender.
2. Sprinkle **coconut flakes** on top to garnish. Done!

3. Watermelon strawberry smoothie (vegan)

Nutrition per serving:	KCAL	FAT	CARBS	PROTEIN
	211	5g	34.5g	9.5g

2 cups soy milk (2 cups = 500ml)
1 ½ cups watermelon (1 ½ cups = ca. 200g)
½ cup strawberries (½ cup = 60g)
1 tbsp agave or maple syrup (less if your fruits are sweet and ripe)
3 basil leaves

1. Blend the **soy milk, watermelon, strawberries, syrup** and **basil leaves** together in a blender. That's it!

Open Camembert and Cranberry Sandwich

Vegetarian | Gluten-free option

Servings: 4 | **Total Time:** 6 minutes

Nutrition per serving:	KCAL	FAT	CARBS	PROTEIN
	227	10.5g	27.5g	9g

Ingredients

4 slices of dark bread — nut, or rye for example

12 thin slices of camembert

3 tbsp dried cranberries

3 tbsp walnuts

1 pear

1 cup rocket/arugula

1 tsp butter

Instructions

1. Preheat the oven to 200°C/390°F (if you have a grill function, use that)
2. Chop the **cranberries** and **walnuts** really finely. Slice the **pear** thinly.
3. **Butter** the **bread,** layer the **rocket** on the bottom.
4. Add 3 slices of **camembert** to each slice of bread, then place the pear on top.
5. Sprinkle the cranberries and walnuts on top.
6. Off it goes into the oven until the cheese melts. Done!

Make it gluten-free

You can also pick up your favourite gluten-free bread. Whole Foods should definitely have it, so should any bigger supermarket.

Jansen's pro tip

Use seedless red grapes if you fancy a change to cranberries (or a cheaper option).

Crispbread with Grilled Halloumi and Peas

Vegetarian | Gluten-free option

Servings: 2 crispbreads | **Total Time:** 10 minutes

Nutrition per serving:	KCAL	FAT	CARBS	PROTEIN
	296	20g	11.5g	17g

Ingredients

2 thin slices of halloumi cheese

¼ cup frozen green peas (¼ cup = 50g)

1 tsp butter

2 crispbreads

1 tbsp chervil or dill

2 tbsp creme fraiche

1 tsp lemon juice

Instructions

1. Grill the **halloumi cheese** in a frying pan.
2. Put the **peas** into the pan and gently heat them up, adding a little bit of **butter** and **salt.** This works fine in the microwave too, if you prefer.
3. Chop the **chervil** or **dill leaves** (leave some for garnishing), add them with the **creme fraiche** to a small bowl; season with salt, **pepper** and **lemon juice.**
4. Put the creme fraiche on the **crispbread,** add the peas and finish with the grilled halloumi on top.

Make it gluten-free

Brands like Wasa or Schär offer gluten-free crispbread. Otherwise of course it is not mandatory to use crispbread for this recipe, so feel free to pick your favourite gluten-free bread for this recipe.

Most Awesome Poached Egg Ever

Vegetarian | Gluten-free

Servings: 4 | **Total Time:** 15 minutes

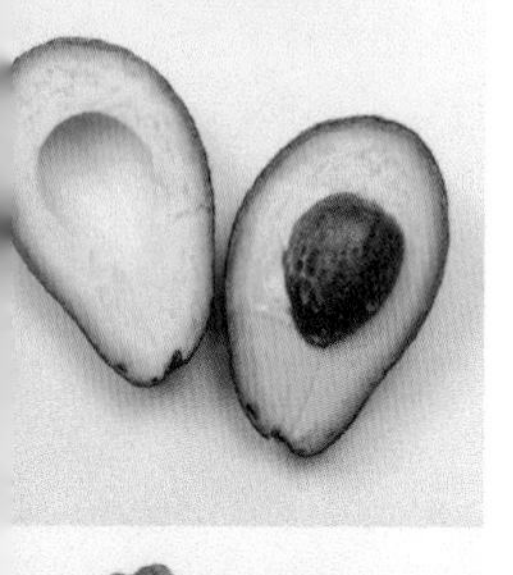

Nutrition per serving:	KCAL	FAT	CARBS	PROTEIN
	289	20.5g	19g	11g

Ingredients

1 avocado

10 cherry tomatoes

6 tbsp cream cheese

4 eggs

2 handfuls fresh baby spinach

4 slices of rye bread (or other dark bread)

Salt and pepper to taste

Instructions

1. Scoop the **avocado** flesh out of the skin with a spoon and mash the flesh in a bowl with **salt** and **pepper.**
2. Cut the **cherry tomatoes** into quarters and add them to the bowl.
3. Put the **cream cheese** into a blender, add the **spinach** and dash of water to get it smooth.
4. Poach the eggs.
5. While the **eggs** are poaching, get your **rye bread** turned into toast — either use the toaster or the oven grill to get them all done in one go.
6. Spread the cream cheese onto the toast, layer the avocado mix on next and top with a poached egg. DELICIOUS!

Make it gluten-free

You can also pick up your favourite gluten-free bread. Whole Foods should definitely have it, so should any bigger supermarket.

Jansen's pro tip

Not sure how to poach an egg? Check out Jamie Oliver's simple but easy way.

Bircher Style Muesli — Summer and Winter Version

Vegan | Gluten-free

Servings: 1 | **Total Time:** 15 minutes

Nutrition per serving *(Summer)*:	KCAL	FAT	CARBS	PROTEIN
	557	22.5g	80g	10.5g

Nutrition per serving *(Winter)*:	KCAL	FAT	CARBS	PROTEIN
	366	4.5g	77g	10g

Ingredients

Summer:

½ cup oats (½ cup = 50g)

⅖ cup coconut milk (⅖ cup = 100ml)

1 kiwi

½ fresh mango

1 tsp coconut flakes

1 tsp agave syrup

Winter:

½ cup oats (½ cup = 50g)

⅖ cup soy milk (⅖ cup = 100ml)

2 tbsp blueberries

2 plums

1 pear

1 tsp agave syrup

Instructions

1. Put the **milk** and the **oats** in a bowl, give them a good stir.

Summer:

1. Chop the **kiwi** and peel the **mango.** See here for a cool mango peeling trick.
2. Add them, the **coconut flakes** and **syrup** to the bowl.
3. Leave everything for 5–10 minutes for desired softness. Enjoy!

Winter:

1. Chop the **plums** and **pear.**
2. Add them, the **blueberry** and **syrup** to the bowl.
3. Leave everything for 5–10 minutes for desired softness. Enjoy!

Jansen's pro tip

Are oats gluten-free? Yes, but they can be contaminated with gluten, because many producers also process wheat, barley and rye in their facilities. So, if you're gluten-intolerant make sure to find oats that are labelled gluten-free to be on the safe side.

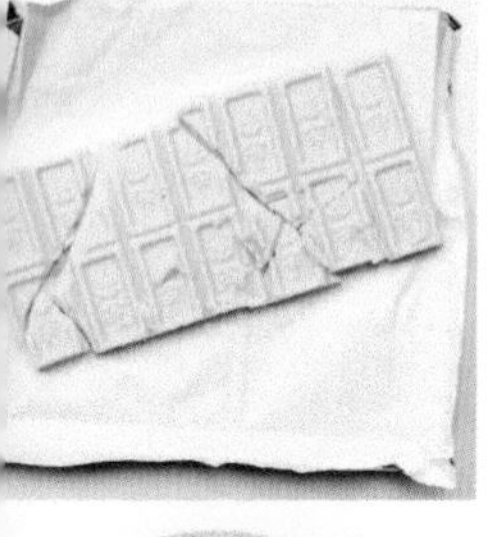

White Chocolate Blueberry Muffins

Vegetarian | Gluten-free

Servings: 6 muffins | **Total Time:** 30 minutes

Nutrition per serving:	KCAL	FAT	CARBS	PROTEIN
	133	6.5g	15.5g	5g

Ingredients

4 eggs

2 ripe bananas

⅓ cup white chocolate (⅓ cup = 60g)

2 tbsp blueberries, fresh or frozen

Instructions

1. Preheat the oven to 180°C/360°F.
2. Mash the **bananas** then mix with **eggs** until they're smooth. A fork or hand blender works just fine.
3. Roughly chop the **chocolate** and add it to the batter, along with the **blueberries.**
4. Add muffin batter to six ramekins, and bake in the preheated oven for 20 minutes at 180°C/360°F.

Oeuf Cocotte with Cream Cheese and Mushrooms

Vegetarian | Gluten-free

Servings: 2 | **Total Time:** 23 minutes

	KCAL	FAT	CARBS	PROTEIN
Nutrition per serving:	150	11.5g	4g	8.5g

Ingredients

2 eggs

2 spring onions

4 mushrooms

4 tbsp cream cheese

1 tsp sambal manis (or your favourite spicy sauce)

1 tsp chopped parsley

Instructions

1. Preheat the oven to 150°C/300°F. Get two small bowls or ramekins ready to use.
2. Thinly chop the **mushrooms** and **spring onions.**
3. Cover the bottom of each ramekin with 2 tbsp of **cream cheese.** Put the mushrooms and springs onions on top of the cream cheese. Drizzle a little **sambal manis** over each. Sprinkle on the **parsley.**
4. Crack an **egg** for each ramekin and gently pour it the top of everything else.
5. Pour some hot water in a different oven dish and place the ramekins in there (au bain marie). Make sure the water covers 50% of the way up the ramekins.
6. Bake for 18 minutes. If the egg is still runny, give it a little longer. Enjoy hot.

Spelt Porridge with Berries

Vegan | Gluten-free option

Servings: 2 | **Total Time:** 10 minutes

	KCAL	FAT	CARBS	PROTEIN
Nutrition per serving:	342	6g	62g	8.5g

Ingredients

¾ cup almond milk (¾ cup = 200ml)

8 tbsp ground spelt

½ cup mixed berries, frozen or fresh (½ cup = 100g)

1 tbsp agave/maple syrup

1 tbsp almonds, roasted

Instructions

1. Boil the **almond milk.**
2. When it begins to boil, drop in the **spelt,** bring it back to the boil once more and then put aside.
3. Throw in the **berries** and **syrup.**
4. Sprinkle the **roasted almonds** on top and enjoy.

Make it gluten-free

Spelt is a grain that contains gluten (bummer). An alternative would be oats that are clearly labelled that they haven't been cross-contaminated with gluten containing products.

Jansen's pro tip

Almond milk can get very pricey. This recipe works well with soy or oat milk too. You could even go for dairy milk, if you like.

Miso Tomatoes with Avocado and Egg

Vegetarian | Gluten-free

Servings: 2 | **Total Time:** 16 minutes

Nutrition per serving:	KCAL	FAT	CARBS	PROTEIN
	512	44.5g	24.5g	11.5g

Ingredients

2 avocados

2 sundried tomatoes

1 tsp miso paste

2 tbsp parsley, chopped

2 eggs

Squeeze of lemon juice

Salt to taste

Instructions

1. Preheat the oven to 180°C/360°F.
2. Cut the **avocados** in half and scoop out the insides. Do your best to leave the skin intact.
3. Cut the avocado flesh into cubes, and do the same with the **sundried tomatoes.**
4. Put the avocado flesh and tomatoes into a bowl, add the miso **paste, parsley, lemon juice** and a little **salt.**
5. Now carefully put everything back into the avocado shells, leaving a big hole in the middle of two of the skins. Crack an **egg** and gently pour it into a hole.
6. Stick it in the oven (use the grill function if you have it) until the egg is cooked — usually around 10–12 minutes. Done!

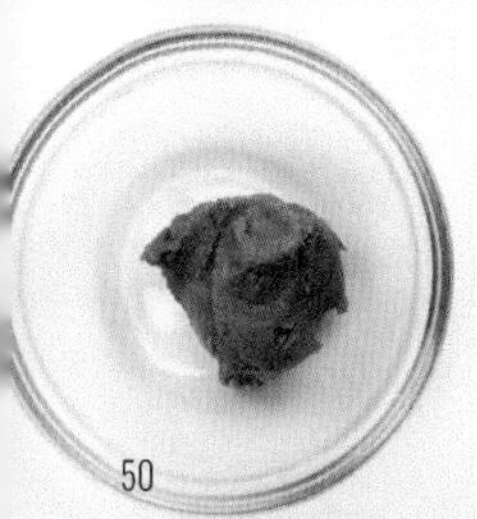

Creamy Breakfast Polenta with Mushrooms

Vegetarian | Gluten-free

Servings: 2 | **Total Time:** 10 minutes

	KCAL	FAT	CARBS	PROTEIN
Nutrition per serving:	359	18.5g	35g	15.5g

Ingredients

2 cups mushrooms (2 cups = 150g)

1 tbsp olive oil

¾ cup cream (¾ cup = 200ml)

⅔ cup water (⅔ cup = 150ml)

½ cup polenta (½ cup = 70g)

2 tbsp pumpkin seeds

½ cup grated cheese like cheddar or vegetarian parmesan

Salt to taste

Instructions

1. Cut the **mushrooms** into quarters, heat up a frying pan with **olive oil** and fry them at high heat.
2. In a separate pot, boil the **cream** and water together with a little **salt.**
3. Once the cream/water mix is boiling, add the **polenta** and reboil for 2 minutes while stirring. You are looking for a soft and creamy polenta.
4. Once it's ready, throw in the **pumpkin seeds** for a little bit of crunch and flavour — give it a final stir.
5. Put it in a bowl and add the mushrooms on top. Finish with some **grated cheese.**

Jansen's pro tip

If something comes up when cooking and you need to reheat the polenta, just add a little more cream and it will go soft again as you reheat.

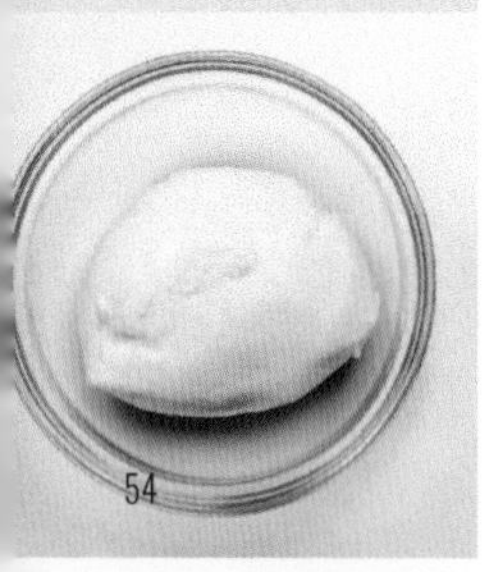

Caprese Quiche with Tomatoes and Basil

Vegetarian | Gluten-free

Servings: 2 | **Total Time:** 20 minutes

Nutrition per serving:	KCAL	FAT	CARBS	PROTEIN
	297	27.5g	5g	10g

Ingredients

2 eggs

⅖ cup cream (⅖ cup = 100ml)

1 tbsp roasted pine nuts

½ tbsp butter

1 medium tomato

8 leaves basil, finely chopped

½ mozzarella ball (½ ball = 60g; make sure you choose a 'vegetarian' mozzarella)

A pinch of salt

Instructions

1. Preheat the oven to 180°C/360°F.
2. Whisk the **eggs** and the **cream** together, add a good pinch of **salt.**
3. Roast the **pine nuts** in a pan until they are golden brown. This should take around two minutes.
4. Take 4 small ramekins and rub their sides and bottom with **butter.**
5. Cut the **tomato** into cubes and add them evenly to each ramekin. Put the **basil** in next, then pour the egg/ cream mixture over it it all.
6. Finally divide the **mozzarella** ball into equal amounts and place a piece in the middle of each ramekin.
7. Sprinkle the pine nuts on top, then put it in the oven for 12 minutes. That's it!

Mango Coconut Smoothie Bowl

Vegan | Gluten-free

Servings: 4 | **Total Time:** 5 minutes

Nutrition per serving:	KCAL	FAT	CARBS	PROTEIN
	341	16g	51g	4.5g

Ingredients

1 ripe mango

1 cup coconut milk (1 cup = 250ml)

2 tbsp popped amaranth (if you can't find popped amaranth, pop it yourself by cooking in a skillet at high heat for a couple of minutes)

2 tbsp agave syrup

⅔ cup white raisins (⅔ cup = 100g)

1 lemon, juiced

Instructions

1. Peel the **mango** and destone.
2. Put the mango, **coconut milk, agave syrup, raisins** and **lemon juice** into the blender.
3. Blend until smooth (there will always be a few bits due to the raisins).
4. Put it in a bowl, sprinkle the **popped amaranth** on top, and enjoy.

Jansen's pro tip

If you're not sure how to peel and destone a mango, check out this cool trick!

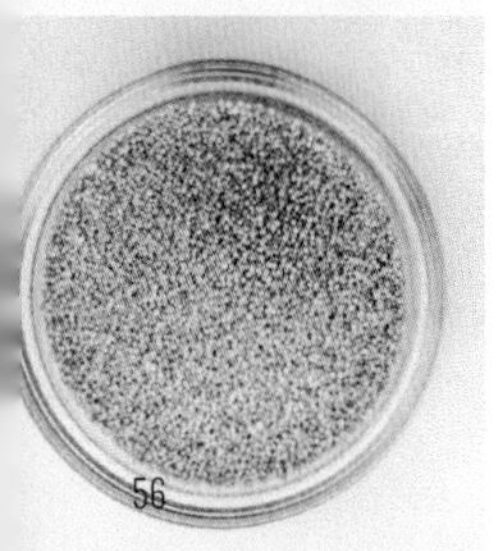

Beautiful Tomato and Feta Omelette

Vegetarian | Gluten-free

Servings: 2 | **Total Time:** 12 minutes

Nutrition per serving:	KCAL	FAT	CARBS	PROTEIN
	294	23g	4.5g	19g

Ingredients

6 eggs

1 tbsp sesame/olive oil or butter

1 cup baby spinach leaves

1 tbsp sundried tomatoes

2 spring onions

2 tbsp crumbled feta cheese (or your favourite cheese)

1 tsp sesame seeds

Instructions

1. Chop the **spinach** and **sundried tomatoes,** thinly slice the **spring onions.**
2. Heat up a big non-stick frying pan on medium, throw some **sesame oil** or a little **butter** in it, and make sure the pan is nicely coated.
3. Whisk the **eggs,** add a little **salt** and **pepper.** Pour **half the egg mixture** in the pan, give it a gentle ruffle/stir and let it fry on medium heat. This is for the first omelette.
4. When the mixture is a little firmer, add **half of the all the ingredients** to it except for the **sesame seeds.**
5. When you feel you can move the omelette fold it once and take it out of the pan. It can be slightly runny when you fold it — it will finish cooking itself on the inside.
6. Repeat steps 4 and 5 for the second omelette.
7. Cut in half, sprinkle with the sesame seeds and enjoy!

Jansen's pro tip

Remember, the inside of the omelette can be slightly 'runny' as you fold it. The egg will finish cooking by itself — this is important for a light, delicate omelette.

Zesty Orange Waffles

Vegetarian | Gluten-free option

Servings: 4–6 waffles | **Total Time:** 25 minutes

	KCAL	FAT	CARBS	PROTEIN
Nutrition per serving:	192	6.5g	29.5g	7g

Ingredients

1 cup spelt flour (1 cup = 150g)
3 tbsp sugar (3 tbsp = 30g)
2 medium organic eggs
1 ½ tbsp butter (1 ½ tbsp = 30g)
¾ cup buttermilk (¾ cup = 200ml)
2 oranges

Instructions

1. Use a fork to mix the **flour** with the **sugar** in a large bowl, then add the **eggs.**
2. Melt the **butter** separately and add to the mixture.
3. Add the **buttermilk** and give it all a good whisk with the fork. Make sure you don't have any clumps. Zest the **orange** (wash and grate the skin) then juice it, and add the **zest** and **juice** to the batter mix.
4. Heat up your waffle machine and pour in the mixture.
5. Bake for 4–5 minutes until golden brown.
6. While the waffles are cooking, peel and chop up **another orange** — the pieces can be used as the topping for the waffle.

Make it gluten-free

Just grab a gluten-free all purpose flour mix. There are various brands like Bob's Red Mill or King Arthur who offer it.

Jansen's pro tip

Instead of a second orange, strawberries make a great summer topping to pair with orange, and thinly sliced pear is perfect for winter.

Tofu Rolls with Pesto and Sundried Tomatoes

Vegetarian | Vegan option

Servings: 4 | **Total Time:** 15 minutes

Nutrition per serving:	KCAL	FAT	CARBS	PROTEIN
	480	24.5g	46.5g	19.5g

Ingredients

4 rolls

8 thin slices of regular or smoked tofu

8 tbsp green or red pesto

4 sun dried tomatoes

4 slices cheddar cheese or vegetarian parmesan

Optional

1 handful cress

Instructions

1. Set the oven to grill or 180°C/360°F
2. Slice the **rolls** and spread the **pesto** on top and bottom. Layer the **tofu** on next, then the **sun dried tomatoes, cheese** and **cress.**
3. Grill in the oven for 3–5 minutes so it's crispy and warm.
4. Enjoy.

Make it vegan

Nowadays you can find various vegan cheese options (even cheddar flavour) in bigger supermarkets. Alternatively, skip the cheese completely and use chargrilled red peppers from a jar as the topping.

Jansen's pro tip

Make your own pesto: Simply blend together 2 cups rocket, ⅓ cup olive oil, 2 tbsp almonds, 1 tbsp lemon juice, salt and pepper. Done!

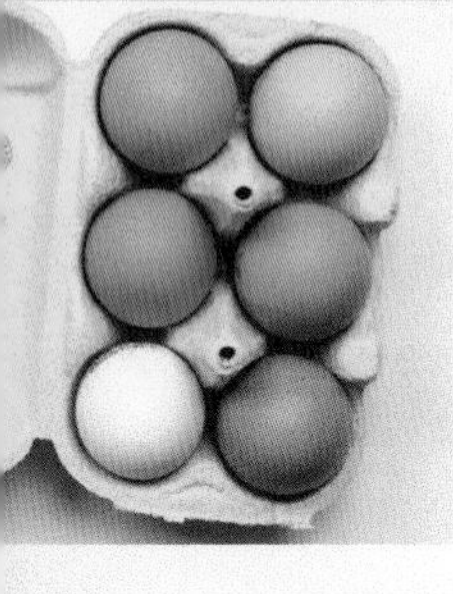

Savoury Pancakes with Parsnips and Almonds

Vegetarian | Gluten-free option

Servings: 2 | **Total Time:** 20 minutes

	KCAL	FAT	CARBS	PROTEIN
Nutrition per serving:	504	24.5g	57.5g	15g

Ingredients

1 tbsp butter
2 eggs
½ cup milk (½ cup = 120ml)
⅘ cup whole wheat flour (⅘ cup = 100g)
½ tsp salt
2 tbsp sour cream
1 parsnip
1 tsp sugar
2 tbsp almonds

Instructions

1. Put the frying pan on the hob and turn it on (low) so it's hot when you need it. Add a little **butter** to the pan.
2. Mix the batter by whisking together the **eggs, milk, flour** and **salt.**
3. Turn the head up to medium and pour out a ladle of batter into the pan and spread it out. Flip after a minute or two once the pancake surface starts to become firm.
4. Peel the skin off the **parsnip** and then discard. Use the peeler to peel the rest of the parsnip into thin strips. Knead it with a dash of **salt** and **sugar** and it will get even softer.
5. Chop some **almonds** and throw them into the mix.
6. Add a little **salt** and **pepper** them to the **sour cream.**
7. Spread some sour cream onto the pancakes and layer over the parsnip and almond.
8. Roll the pancake and cut into 4 equal pieces.

Make it gluten-free

To get the best results we recommend looking for a gluten-free all purpose flour mix. There are various brands like Bob's Red Mill or King Arthur offering it.

Puff Pastry that Rocks

Vegetarian

Servings: 4 | **Total Time:** 30 minutes

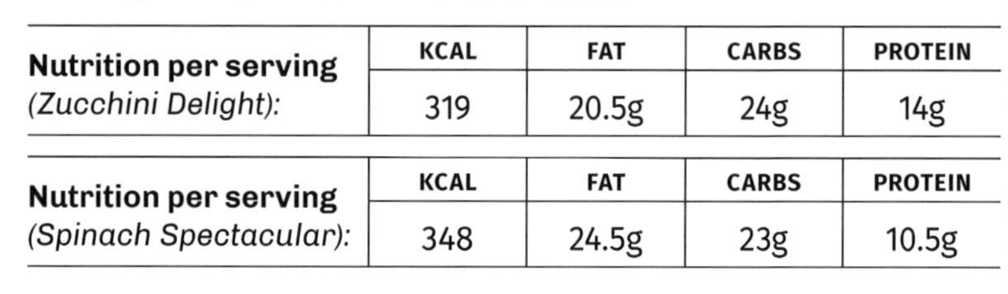

Nutrition per serving *(Zucchini Delight):*	KCAL	FAT	CARBS	PROTEIN
	319	20.5g	24g	14g

Nutrition per serving *(Spinach Spectacular):*	KCAL	FAT	CARBS	PROTEIN
	348	24.5g	23g	10.5g

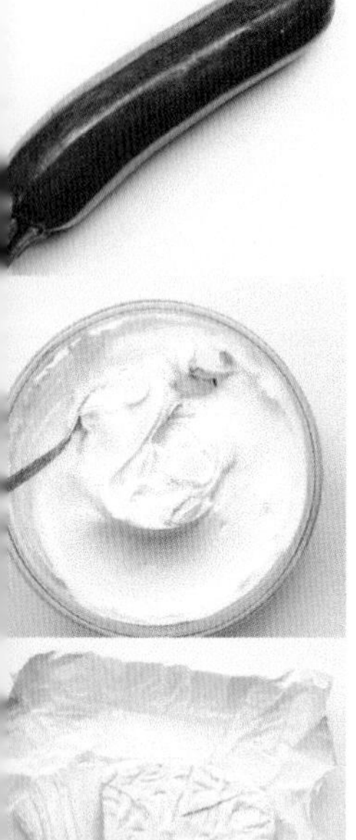

Ingredients

Version 1 — Zucchini Delight

1 sheet puff pastry

1 cup mascarpone (1 cup = 250ml)

1 medium zucchini

½ cup basil leaves

Salt and pepper to taste

Version 2 — Spinach Spectacular

1 sheet puff pastry

12–15 thin slices brie

2 cups baby spinach

3 tbsp almonds, roughly chopped

Salt and pepper to taste

Instructions

1. Heat up the oven to 180°C/360°F.
2. Roll out the **puff pastry** and half it.

Version 1

1. Roughly chop the **basil leaves** and mix them into the **mascarpone.** Now spread the mix onto one half of the pastry.
2. Grate the **zucchini** and layer it on top of the mascarpone mix.
3. Add **salt** and **pepper** to taste.
4. Sprinkle a little bit of water on the edges and put the other half of pastry on top, close it tightly (press down with a fork around the edges).
5. Bake for 18 minutes until the pastry is golden brown. Enjoy!

Version 2

1. Layer the **brie** onto one half of the pastry. Make sure most of the pastry is covered.
2. Add the **spinach** and **chopped almonds** on top of the brie.
3. Add **salt** and **pepper** to taste.
4. Sprinkle a little bit of **water** on the edges and put the other half of pastry on top, close it tightly (press down with a fork around the edges).
5. Bake for 18 minutes until the pastry is golden brown. Enjoy!

Decadent Ricotta Croissants with Honey and Lemon

Vegetarian

Servings: 2 | **Total Time:** 6 minutes

Nutrition per serving:	KCAL	FAT	CARBS	PROTEIN
	435	15g	51.5g	10g

Ingredients

⅕ cup ricotta or mascarpone cheese (⅕ cup = 50g)

½ lemon, juiced and zested

2 croissants

2 tbsp honey

1 handful roasted walnuts, crushed

2 tsp your favourite jam

Instructions

1. Mix the **ricotta** or **mascarpone cheese** with the **lemon juice** and **zest.**
2. Cut the **croissant** lengthwise and spread the cheese over one side.
3. Drizzle some **honey** over the cheese, and sprinkle a few **crushed nuts** on top.
4. Spread your favourite **jam** on the other side.
5. Close the croissant back together and you are good to go for one mega tasty breakfast.

Jansen's pro tip

The earlier you get yourself out of bed and to the bakery, the fresher the croissants will be ;-) Also, there can be big difference in the quality of honey, so when possible, look for something local and handmade.

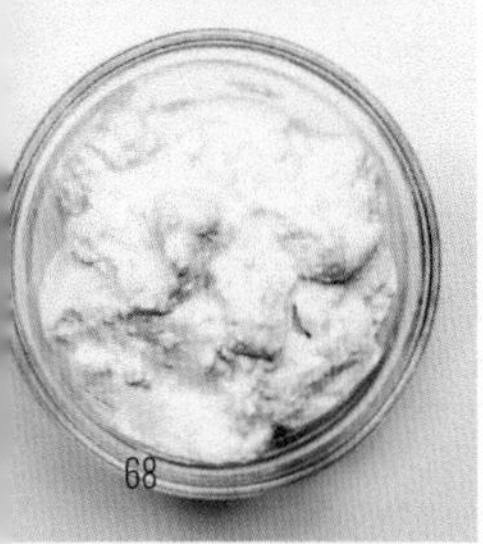

Disclaimer

Great care has been taken to provide accurate nutritional information with each recipe. However, please note it is for guideline purposes only and we make no guarantee as to the accuracy of this information. Please consult a doctor before making any decisions about treatment of any conditions you may have, or think you may have.

Thanks

**FOR READING,
AND AS ALWAYS THANKS
FOR YOUR SUPPORT.**

Enjoy breakfast!

Annex

1. Vegetarian, GF option, Vegan Opt — Cheddar and Fig Melt — 4 ingredients, 10 minutes, 15g protein per serving (260 kcal), 24g on 400 kcal
2. Vegetarian, GF option, Vegan Opt, — Mediterranean Pitas with Feta and Honey, 6 ingredients, 18 minutes, 6g protein per serving (220 kcal), 10.9g on 400 kcal
3. Vegetarian, Vegan Opt, GF Opt — Indian Parathas with Curried Carrots, 6 ingredients, 18 minutes, 3.3g protein per serving (110 kcal), 12g on 400 kcal
4. Vegetarian, Vegan Opt, GF Opt — French Coconut Toast with Blueberries, 5 ingredients, 18 minutes, 4.3g protein per serving (181 kcal), 9.5g on 400 kcal
5. Vegetarian, Vegan Opt, GF — Sweet Potato and Parsnip Hash Browns, 6 ingredients, 12 minutes, 5.8g protein per serving (313 kcal), 7.4g on 400 kcal
6. Vegetarian, GF, Vegan Opt — Grilled Tomatoes with Blueberry Jam, 4 ingredients, 20 minutes, 2.9g protein per serving (75 kcal), 15.5g on 400 kcal
7. Vegetarian, GF, Vegan Opt — Fried Chickpeas with Zucchini and Yoghurt, 5 ingredients, 12 minutes, 15.6g protein per serving (433 kcal), 15g on 400 kcal
8. Vegetarian, GF, Vegan Opt — Chia Pomegranate Yoghurt, 6 ingredients, 20 minutes, 17.1g protein per serving (306 kcal), 22.3g on 400 kcal
9. Vegetarian, GF Opt — Fresh Mexican Style Breakfast Wraps, 6 ingredients, 6 minutes, 14.8g protein per serving (379 kcal), 16g on 400 kcal
10. Vegetarian, GF Opt — Open Camembert and Cranberry Sandwich, 6 ingredients, 6 minutes, 8.8g protein per serving (227 kcal), 15.5g on 400 kcal
11. Vegetarian, GF Opt — Grilled Halloumi and Peas on Crispbread, 6 ingredients, 10 minutes, 17.2g protein per serving (296 kcal), 23.2g on 400 kcal
12. Vegetarian, GF Opt — Most Awesome Poached Egg Ever, 6 ingredients, 15 minutes, 11g protein per serving (289 kcal), 15.2g on 400 kcal
13. Vegetarian, GF — White chocolate blueberry muffins, 4 ingredients, 20 minutes, 4.7g protein per serving (133 kcal), 14.1g on 400 kcal
14. Vegetarian, GF — Oeuf Cocotte with Cream Cheese and Mushrooms, 6 ingredients, 23 minutes, 8.5g protein per serving (150 kcal), 22.5g on 400 kcal

15. Vegetarian, GF — Miso Tomatoes with Avocado and Egg, 6 ingredients, 16 minutes, 11.2g protein per serving (512 kcal), 8.7g on 400 kcal
16. Vegetarian, GF — Creamy Breakfast Polenta with Mushrooms, 5 ingredients, 10 minutes, 15.7g protein per serving (359 kcal), 16.5g on 400 kcal
17. Vegetarian, GF — Caprese Quiche with Tomatoes and Basil, 6 ingredients, 20 minutes, 10g protein per serving (297 kcal), 13.4g on 400 kcal
18. Vegetarian, GF — Beautiful Tomato Feta Omelette, 6 ingredients, 20 minutes, 19.2g protein per serving (294 kcal), 26.2g on 400 kcal
19. Vegetarian GF Opt — Zesty Orange Waffles, 4 ingredients, 25 minutes, 6.8g protein per serving (192 kcal), 13g on 400 kcal
20. Vegetarian, Vegan Opt — Tofu Rolls with Pesto and Sundried Tomatoes, 5 ingredients, 15 minutes, 19.2g protein per serving (480 kcal), 16g on 400 kcal
21. Vegetarian — Savoury Pancakes with Parsnips and Almonds, 6 ingredients, 20 minutes, 13.9g protein per serving (419 kcal), 14g on 400 kcal
22. Vegetarian — Puff Pastry that Rocks, 4 ingredients, 30 minutes, v1 10.5g protein per serving (319 kcal), v2 10.5g protein per serving (348 kcal), 12g on 400 kcal
23. Vegetarian — Decadent Ricotta Croissants with Honey and Lemon, 6 ingredients, 6 minutes, 10.2g protein per serving (440 kcal), 9g on 400 kcal
24. Vegan, GF Opt — Crepes with Chocolate and Coconut, 6 ingredients, 20 minutes, 10.1g protein per serving (404 kcal), 10g on 400 kcal
25. Vegan, GF — Tropical Quinoa Porridge, 5 ingredients, 30 minutes, 8.2g protein per serving (435 kcal), 7.5g on 400 kcal
26. Vegan, GF — Tangy Arepas with Pomegranate and Lime, 6 ingredients, 30 minutes, 4.1g protein per serving (290 kcal), 5.6g on 400 kcal
27. Vegan, GF — Mango Coconut Smoothie Bowl, 6 ingredients, 5 minutes, 4.4g protein per serving (341 kcal), 5g on 400 kcal
28. Vegan, GF — Fruity Vegan Smoothies, 5 ingredients, 2 minutes, 9.3g protein per serving (211 kcal), 6.6g protein per serving (330 kcal) 9.5g protein per serving (215 kcal), 18g on 400 kcal
29. Vegan, GF — Bircher Style Muesli — Summer and Winter Version, 6 ingredients, 15 minutes, winter 10.5g protein per serving (557 kcal) summer 9.8 protein per serving (366 kcal), 10.7g on 400 kcal
30. Vegan — Spelt Porridge with Berries, 5 ingredients, 10 minutes, 8.3g protein per serving (342 kcal), 9.7g on 400 kcal

BREAKFAST IN *Six*

Printed in Great Britain
by Amazon